HOT P

EASY GUIDE ON HOW TO GROW HOT PEPPERS

By Lucky James

Table of Contents

Chapter one: Introduction

The high consumption of pepper today has led to a lot of people venturing into pepper farming. In the world today hot pepper is been consume domestically by a lot of household. Hot pepper is been use for the preparation of different kinds of meal. Today hot pepper has played an important role in some economy in the area of exporting it to the international market. According to agriculturist hot pepper belongs to the family of genus Capsicum of the Solanaceae. History also told us that hot pepper originated from American region, then later spread to the whole world. Today hot pepper is use everywhere in the world for food ingredients and also for medicinal properties. According to agricultural specialist hot pepper contains some substances called capsaicinoids. One of the things that is responsible for the spiciness of hot peppers is capsaicin. Inside the pepper, the area of the placenta is the hottest part of the pepper. Another thing again that provides a feeling of heat is the seed, which are in contact with the placenta of the pepper fruit. Let us look at some of the health benefit of hot pepper. The following are some of the health benefit of hot pepper.

1. According health practitioners the Capsaicin in hot peppers helps to stop the growth of prostate cancer cells.

2. Another benefit of hot pepper is that hot peppers are very rich in potassium and folic acid and also it does not contain sodium or carbohydrates.
3. Hot peppers also can be used to treat the following; migraines, arthritis, and muscular pains. Because it contains an anti-inflammatory properties.
4. Stuffy head and nose can be cleared up using hot peppers. It is very clear that adding more pepper in soup can help to fight the following; colds, sinusitis, and bronchitis.
5. Another health benefit of hot peppers is that it helps to improve blood circulation and also it increases the strength of the arteries.
6. One of the things you can use to combat depression is hot peppers.
7. It is said that a dried up hot pepper can be used to heal wounds. Because it can kill the bacteria's inside the wound.

Chapter two: Different varieties of hot pepper

On this chapter we are going to look at the varieties of hot peppers. The following are some of the varieties of hot peppers:

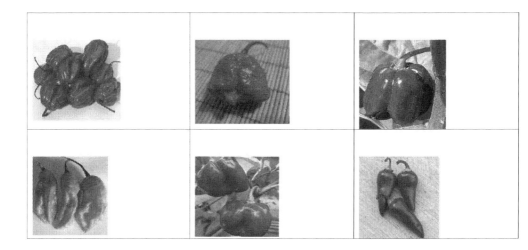

1. Golden nugget hot peppers: One thing about this variety of pepper is that they are very productive. The fruit of this particular variety of pepper ripen to golden yellow. Below is the image of it.

2. The Jwala Finger Hot Pepper: This particular variety of hot pepper is the most popular hot pepper that is grow in Indian. Below is the image of this variety.

3. The Italian Sweet hot Pepper: This variety of pepper is also refer to as frying pepper. The Italians always use this pepper for cooking: below is the image of this variety of hot pepper.

4. The Melrose Pepper: Another good variety of pepper is the Melrose pepper. Below is the image of the Melrose pepper.

5. The hot Banana Pepper: The hot banana pepper is also known as the yellow wax pepper. The hot banana pepper is a medium-sized pepper that has a mild, sweet taste. Below is the image of hot banana pepper.

6. The Trinidad Perfume Pepper: This particular variety is not too hot. The Trinidad perfume pepper is a habanero type and it also produces pods similar to a typical orange habanero pepper. Below is the image of the variety.

7. The hot Paprika Supreme Pepper: One thing about this pepper is that it is very good when dried and ground, this pepper can be used to make powdered spices. Below is the image of Paprika Supreme Pepper.

8. The cherry hot pepper: This particular variety of pepper is very succulent and aromatic. Below is the image of the pepper.

9. The Shishito hot Pepper: This particular variety is a Japanese pepper. This particular pepper is small. Below is the image of the Shishito hot Pepper.

10. The Hungarian Black hot Pepper: These particular varieties are mildly hot and also have a delicious flavor. Below is the image.

11. Tiger Teeth hot peppers: This particular Pepper is very hot and they turn from green, to orange, then to red when they are finally mature. Below is the image of the pepper.

All these peppers mention are the major varieties of hot pepper.

Chapter three: Land Preparation for Hot Pepper Planting

Before you consider planting your hot peppers the following are what you really need to take into consideration about the site and the land.

1. Make sure that the land is very free from flood. One thing about hot pepper is that they cannot tolerate water logging conditions.
2. The site should be located in a place where there is access to water and good road. This good road will ensure a proper usage of machinery for land preparation and transportation.
3. Try and ensure that the land is located in a place where security is guaranteed.

The preparation of the land

The following are what you need to do to prepare the land for planting:

1. Try and ensure that you clear all the trees and stumps.
2. There should be a minimal disposal of the top soil.
3. Ensure that the soil is deep ploughed (Chiseled) at a depth of about 18-24 inches.
4. Make sure you apply limestone at the rate of 1-2 tons/acre, this will help to reduce soil acidity.
5. Ensure you Construct a Cambered beds with dimensions of 1.5 ft high x 6-10ft wide.
6. To ensure the removal of excess water, drains (2ft – 2.5ft deep) should be constructed.

Chapter four: preparation of seed for planting

The following are the steps on the preparation of seeds for planting from the fresh (berries) fruits.

1. The first thing to do is to remove the flesh of the half ripe or ripe pepper from around the seeds still attached at the center.
2. After that the seed should be placed in a bucket fully submerged in water. It should be stirred gently, make sure this is done at least 2 times per day.

3. In three days' time the seed will finally detached from the centre. The next thing you will do is to drain the water out carefully allowing the seeds to finally settle down at the bottom.
4. Make that you did not place the seed directly to sunlight, but allow it to dry by natural air.
5. After one month the viability of the seed will start decreasing.

Before the seedling should be transplant to the field, the seedling should be at least four to six weeks old.

Chapter five: Pepper planting and spacing

Planting of the pepper: Before transplanting the seedlings ensure that it is about 4-6 weeks old. Make sure you also carry out the transplanting in the afternoon. If you want to plant the seedling, place it in a hole that is filled with a well cured manure. This well cured manure will cover the root system. When planting, try and be very careful to avoid damage to the roots. Try and drenched the transplanted seedling with soil insecticide like Fastac. Fastac is a very good protective treatment. Fastac can also help to prevent attack from mole cricket. Below is an image of a mole cricket.

Another thing that will encourage good rooting is the application of fertilizer. Examples of fertilizer to apply are 10:52:10 or 12:24:12.

Spacing the pepper plant: The following are what you need to consider when spacing the pepper plant; the variety, the soil type, the inputs available. Try and consider the recommended distance, this will help to prevent competition between plants, it will also help to reduce soil surface for weed growth. If you actually wants to achieve a maximum production, a specialize irrigation system is required in a higher planting densities.

The following are planting spacing in pepper:

If for example you are growing the peppers in a single-dug bed (soil prepared to 8-10"—20-25 cm), make sure you set the pepper plants on 16-18" (40-45 cm) apart in rows 24-30" (61-76 cm) apart.

If for example you are growing the peppers in a deep-dug or raised garden bed (soil prepared to a depth of 20-24"—51-61cm), make sure you set the pepper plants on 16-18" (40-45 cm) centers (plants 16-18"—40-45 cm—apart in all directions).

Chapter six: How to apply fertilizer

Putting fertilizer on your pepper plants depends on how develop your pepper plant is. In the area of fertilizing peppers moderation is the key. Which means you have to be extremely very careful. Make sure you don't fertilize the peppers the on the first week of transplant. Most especially don't fertilize the pepper plants with fertilizers that contain high level of nitrogen. If you mistakenly fertilize the pepper plants with a fertilizer that contain high level of nitrogen it can cause abundance of green growth and also lead to a very little fruit production. For you to fertilize your pepper plants wait until the plants produce blossoms, then you can now fertilize the plant. One thing about pepper plant is that several different types fertilizers can be used to fertilize them. Whenever you purchase a fertilizer you want to use to fertilize your pepper plant make sure you pay attention to the 3 number code on the fertilizer. The meaning of these 3 number code actually indicate the amount of nitrogen, phosphate and potassium that are actually contained in that particular fertilizer you want to purchase and use. For example 10-10-10 fertilizer contains the following; 10% nitrogen, 10% phosphate and 10% potassium. Then if you look at 5-10-10 fertilizer bag it contains 5% percent nitrogen. While the 10-5-10 fertilizer bag contains the following; 10% nitrogen, 5% phosphate and 10% potassium. It is strongly advice that, if you want to fertilize your peppers, try and look for 5-10-10 fertilizer. The reason while is because this fertilizer contains half as much nitrogen as phosphate and potassium. If the phosphate and potassium are higher in number it will encourage more fruit production. While if the nitrogen is lower in number it will really help the pepper plant to grow. Under normal condition granular fertilizers are applied at a rate of 1 1/2 pounds per 100 square feet. If for instance you want to fertilize your pepper plants with granular fertilizer make sure you don't let the granules touch the plant. If the granules touches the plant it may burn the plant. If you really want to apply a granular fertilizer on the pepper plant you can apply it in a circle, then after that you water the pepper plants very well.

If for example you want to use a water soluble fertilizer (a method of dissolving the fertilizer in water and use a spray) make sure you don't spray the fertilizer on top of the pepper plants. When spraying try as much as possible to concentrate your efforts at the base of the pepper plant.

Also it is strongly advice that after fertilizing the pepper plants, try to apply a layer of mulch around the pepper plants. The reason while you need to apply a layer of mulch is that it will help to prevent the evaporation of moisture from the soil. Applying a layer of mulch will also help to control weeds on the pepper plants.

Chapter seven: Pest control in pepper farming

On this chapter we are going to look at some of the pest that attack pepper and how to control it. The following are some of the major pest that attack pepper:

1. The mole cricket: The mole cricket is one of the pests that attack pepper. The mole cricket attacks the seedling by cutting the

stem under the soil surface. One of the ways to control it is by using soil insecticide like Fastac. Below is the image of the mole cricket.

2. The aphids: Aphids really serve as a vector of viral disease. Aphids can be control using soil insecticide biological. The following are what you can use; Neem products, Pegasus, etc. below is the image of Aphids.

3. The cut worm: Cut worm is another pest that attacks pepper. Cut worm eats the leaves of the pepper. Cut worm can be control biological by using Dipel DF Pegasus, pirate, etc. Below is the image of cut worm.

4. The white flies: White fly is another pest that attack pepper. They are vector for viral disease. They can be control by using Pegasus, pirate, etc. below is the image of white flies.

5. The Thrips: Thrips is another pest that attack pepper. They can also be control by using Pegasus, pirate, etc. below is the image of thrips.

6. The mites: Mites are pest that damage the leaves of the pepper. They can also be control using Pegasus, pirate, etc. Below is the image of mites.

Chapter eight: Disease control in pepper farming

On this chapter we are going to look at some of the disease in pepper and how to control it. The following are some of the diseases in pepper.

1. Bacterial wilt disease: This particular disease is caused by the bacterium Erwinia tracheiphila.

This disease is very destructive most especially in hot and wet season. The symptoms of this disease are Discoloration of vascular tissues, Sudden wilting of plant, etc. one of the ways this disease can spread round is through a contaminated equipment and tools. Another way this disease can spread round is through rain splash. The following are ways you can control this disease; by liming of Soil, by rogueing of diseased plants, by Crop Rotation.

2. The Phythophtora Root Rot (Fungal): Another destructive disease that affect pepper is Phythophtora Root Rot (Fungal) disease.

Some of the symptoms of this disease on the pepper are dark brown lesions on the stems, also the pepper will be experiencing loss of leaves. This disease can spread round through some of the infected seed. The following are ways to control this disease; There should a proper Drainage, Proper crop rotation Acrobat, etc.

3. Pepper bacterial Spot: This particular disease is the most important disease affecting pepper.

The symptoms of this disease are tiny brown irregular spots on leaves, and also on the stem, the flowers and the pepper fruits. This disease can spread through Seed / soil borne. This disease can be control by using copper based fungicide. An example of copper based fungicide is Kocide.

4. Pepper Blossom End Rot: This particular disease is a physiological disorder which causes a dark, sunken area on the lower end of peppers, the symptoms include a dark leathery spotting at the blossom end of the pepper.

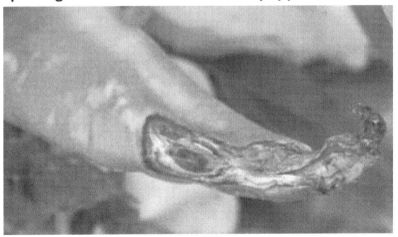

This disease can spread if there is inadequate calcium on the pepper plant. One the ways to control this disease is by applying fertilizer that contains calcium at the early stage of growth of the pepper.

5. Pepper Anthracnose (Fungus): This disease is another fungal disease that affects pepper.

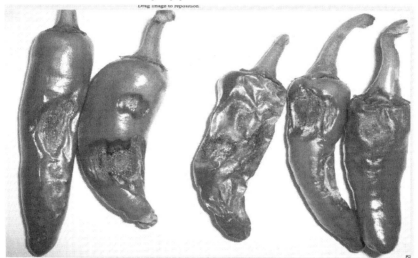

This disease can spread through wind and water. One of the ways to observe the symptoms of this disease is there will be a small sunken water soaked lesions on the pepper fruit. This disease can be control through crop rotation, and the use of copper based fungicides.

Chapter nine: Hot pepper harvest and storage

On this chapter we are going to look at how to harvest hot peppers and how to store them.

Harvesting hot peppers

Harvesting hot pepper actually depends on the varieties and what you want to use them for.

There are some peppers that can be harvested when they are green, an example of such pepper are Jalapeno peppers. Other peppers that can be harvest when they are green are like Anaheim," or New Mexico, chili peppers. All these peppers mention can also be used when they are fresh, canned or roasted. Some of the peppers that can be harvested when they are ripe to their mature color of red or yellow are Habanero" and cherry hot peppers. Whenever you want to harvest the pepper make sure you harvest them during dry weather. If you want to harvest them cut them from the stem, it is better than picking them. Under normal condition hot peppers ripen 70- 85 days. In some case it can take up to 150 days from the time of transplanting. Peppers matured when they have actually reach their full size. Try as much as possible to be very careful when harvesting them. If you are not careful in harvesting them nicks and bruises can actually cause them to rot very quickly.

Hot peppers storage

One thing about hot peppers is that they are full of water and they can decay or dry out rapidly.

After harvesting the pepper make sure that you don't wash them, but you can brush any dirt on them. What you have to do immediately is to store them in a produce bin of your refrigerator. One thing about hot peppers is that they do very well at temperatures between 40 and 45 degrees Fahrenheit. If you can actually store them this way they will last for 2 or 3 weeks. Anytime you are handling or cutting hot pepper make sure that you always wear rubber glove because hot peppers has volatile oils that can burn your eyes and skin.

HOT PEPPERS

EASY GUIDE ON HOW TO GROW HOT PEPPERS

By Lucky James

Made in United States
Troutdale, OR
01/25/2024